Poems from the

Poems from the Unconscious

Reflections on Trauma, Recovery and Healing

Phil O'Neill

Copyright ©Phil O'Neill 2022
All rights reserved. No part of this publication may be reproduced, distributed, or transmitted in any form or by any means, including photocopying, recording, or other electronic or mechanical methods, without the prior written permission of the publisher, except in the case of brief quotations embodied in critical reviews and certain other non-commercial uses permitted by copyright law.

The right of Phil O'Neill to be identified as the author of this work has been asserted by him in accordance with the Copyright, Designs and Patents Act 1988.

Phil O'Neill, Author

Father, Grandfather, Internationalist who lived for ten years in France, one in Italy and three in California. He has visited more than sixty countries. He was a frustrated poet while pursuing a successful professional business career. Despite writing poetry since a young child and being a prize-winner in a National Creative Writing competition, aged fifteen, he was late to the craft. His first short story was published in a regional newspaper in 2010, his first published poem in 2017.

He has a bachelor's degree in International Marketing from the University of Greenwich, an MBA from the London Business School, and he finally fulfilled his dream when he studied for an MA in Creative Writing at the University of Kent in Paris 2017, graduating at sixty three years of age. Phil lives in Kent, England, with Sveta, but travels the world as much as he can, meeting and making friends and visiting family.

Agatha O'Neill, Artist

Cambridge graduate, Central St. Martins, Accademia di Belle Arti di Roma. Artist, Designer, Mum, Daughter. A gifted collaborator who enhances her father's poetry with amazing illustrations. Agatha encouraged Phil to be more ambitious and publish this book, rather than the pamphlet he originally planned.

Agatha also lives in Kent, England, with her beautiful boy Theo.

Instagram: @agatha_creative
www.agathaoneill.com

To my wonderful, departed, saintly parents, Tom and Gwyn, who did what they could.

To my older brother, Bernard, who has survived and will read these poems.

To my cousins, especially Julie and Judith, who do what they can and have worked so hard, with love, to keep us together as a family.

To my former wife and mother of my three eldest daughters, Clotilde, who did what she could.

To my beautiful daughters Julia, Clara, Agatha and Katya. I am so proud of you. I was born in the Valleys of South Wales. We are now a global family with seven fluent languages and five nationalities between us. You inspire me every day with your love, creativity, and goodness. I know where you are and love you with my all. Forgive me. I did what I could.

To my wonderful grandchildren who embrace the world without fear: Lilya, Theo, Mia and Tom.

To my wife and muse, Sveta, mother of Katya, thank you for believing in me and my poetry. I can achieve anything with your love and support.

Acknowledgements

My tutor, Dorothy Lehane, at the University of Kent who encouraged me to find my voice and to write about my family.

My fellow student, the beautiful poet Jane Hartshorn, who shared some wonderful creative moments with me in Paris.

My amazing, tolerant, supportive friends who have encouraged, cajoled, advised me: Mark Lacey, Ian MacLeod, Martin Prentice, Alastair Scarborough.

Special thanks to Andrew Dawson for his efforts in editing my words. Of course, all errors remain mine and mine alone.

Foreword

I have known Phil O'Neill for thirty years, but never quite realised the epic journey of self-discovery that he had undertaken, which he has captured in all its rawness in this collection of poetry. How common is that sense of knowing someone well enough, but maybe not exploring those hidden facets of their lives, of our lives, that make us who we are, shape us and our destiny? Sometimes we choose not to present our emotional selves to others because we fear their reactions, or we don't feel others will understand or be interested.

Until recently, I worked on a campaign that had been running for almost fifteen years and had at its heart "champions" – people with a variety of mental health problems. They agreed to speak openly about their issues so that society might change the way it thought about and reacted to those who have experienced poor mental health. Together, we created an environment in which these conversations could take place that was as free of stigma and discrimination as we could make it. Although the campaign has ceased, owing to lack of funding, the social movement that was created will empower people to continue to talk about mental health, and their experience of it in ways that feel comfortable to them. In Phil's case, this has been through a lifetime of writing poetry, with many of those poems presented for the first time in this book.

Not being confident to talk about feelings, fearing the negative reactions of others, of being rejected, being belittled or disbelieved, leads so many people to bury their distress as deeply as they can. I know that this isn't the solution. I know the damaging impact of not finding the words to articulate what's going on inside us, or the confidence to externally express them, the resultant internalising of shame; that there must be something fundamentally wrong with our very being if we feel like this.

Sharing our stories, through whatever medium, is a powerful vehicle with which we reach those who might be experiencing, or have experienced, mental illness. It allows us to take comfort in knowing that we are not alone, and that our mental distress is simply one feature of what makes us who we are. It helps us reach those who are unaware of close family, friends or acquaintances who may be in need of support by demonstrating what living with mental illness actually looks and feels like, as opposed to some of the more sensationalist portrayals on television and other media. Sharing stories builds empathy.The words the poet chooses to lay down can be cathartic; a way to convey what's going on in our unconscious without the burden of the spoken word. I believe Phil has achieved that in this book. In reading this collection, the power in his words comes not just from what they meant to him, but from the deep emotional connection that you, the reader, make as you read the poems in the light of your own experience.

My hope for this book of poems is that it's read as a reminder of the importance of articulating how we feel, of having honest and open conversations about the topic of mental health and our own experience within it. I hope that it will inspire others to find comfort and perhaps a way to express their own feelings. I hope it will motivate all to hear what others have to say and to think differently about those who have ever settled, for however long, in a dark place.

Jo Loughran
Director Time to Change (2016-2021)

Some of the content deals with aspects of abuse, neglect and suicide, and some readers may find that it triggers painful memories.
If you are affected by any of these issues, please seek help from your own support network or call Samaritans free on 116 123 or email jo@samaritans.org

Contents

Introduction 1

Trans-Generational Trauma 10

    Origins of Trauma 11

        Home 11

        Grandfather 13

        Grandmother: "A Lovely Wreath" 16

        Bank Farm, Hope Valley, Shropshire 20

        Three Blind Mice 23

        Where Are the Children? 24

        Betty 26

        Dad 29

        Faith Lost 30

        A Tribute to Dennis 32

    The Ripple Effect 34

        There Was an Old Woman 34

        Childhood 35

        Dennis Speaks 40

        Lament for Dennis 42

Depression 44

    Comb 45

    How Close? 46

    A Long Time Ago 47

Gallery 48

Plea 49

If Only 50

Solitude 51

Tears 53

Ten Years 54

The Black Horse 55

It Really Hurts 56

Thanks 57

Self Abuse 58

Trying so Hard to Ignore the Chimera on My Back 59

Poèmes Français 1992 - French Poems 1992 64

Compréhension - Understanding 65

La Vie Fade - Dull Life 66

Amour Perdu - Lost Love 67

Tu es là - You are there 68

Suicide, Self-Harm, Survival 70

Mutual Understanding 71

The Whole Circle 72

The Psychiatrist 73

Escape 74

When I Was Sixty-Four 75

A Meeting 76

I Will Die Happy 77

Money Talks 80

Addiction 82

Look after Yourself 84

Catharsis 85

Healing **92**

The Choice 93

Coping 94

Black Ball 95

Greatest Love 96

Poet 97

Comfort 98

Discomfort 99

American Dreams 100

The Drunken Juggler 102

Deserving 103

Do Not Cry for Me 104

The Old Lovers 105

The Sense of You 106

Solitude **108**

The Artist's Lot 109

The Power of Art 110

Renaissance 114

    The Universe Pauses as Infinite Love Expands 115

    An Elegy to My Father 116

    Father's Advice 117

    Julia is free 118

    Family Love 120

    To My Muse 121

    Forty Foot Drop 122

    Not Much Time 124

    GHOTI 125

    The Simple Truth 126

    One Month Short of His Sixtieth Birthday 127

    Whole Again 128

The Beginning 129

Further Reading 132

Introduction

In the early 1990s, I was a successful international marketing executive and a happy family man. Out of nowhere, I became submerged in a debilitating mental health crisis. I was referred by my G.P. to a Harley Street psychiatrist as my life unravelled. I became a mess. Riddled with despair, my behaviour descended into extreme self-destructiveness (alcohol, sex), helplessness, an inability to work, and disruptive social interactions. I spent days in bed. I neglected my family, my work and my home, all of which eventually led to the collapse of my marriage.

Many accounts of depression cite a specific event, such as a relationship breakdown, where the psychological response is disproportionate. My experience was the exact opposite; my depression caused mayhem. It was clear to my doctor and psychiatrist there was something more profoundly amiss than a response to an experience. I had combatted mental health issues on several occasions in my life. This one was huge with the worst of bouts and no discernible cause. It led to consequences that could be life threatening.

During two years of treatment, my psychiatrist helped me start the healing process. I then decided to embark on a psychotherapeutic path to build upon my new-found core of well-being. I believe talking therapy is so important. It's always better to seek professional help. A cliché perhaps, but would you ask a friend to fix a broken leg? I thought therapy would give me the strength to protect myself from future tribulations. I learned techniques to control episodes of depression, but they didn't feel authentic. I always doubted that I was bi-polar ("manic-depressive" as diagnosed by a G.P. while still at school). There were still many times when I felt a complete loss of control where I was bed-ridden, engulfed in profound sadness. Alcohol and dispiriting sexual activities continued to destroy my self-worth.

Finally, I felt comfortable with a diagnosis that my mental ill-health was due to childhood trauma or indeed, and more likely, trans-generational trauma.

This confirmed my thesis that depression, possibly "inherited", caused destruction and pain rather than being the result of a specific, extraneous, contemporary event. This made me worried for my daughters. Would I pass on the trauma? My psychiatrist often asked me: "Where are the children?"

I had always wondered why my close family seemed to suffer more than most from disruptive behaviour, addictions, relationship problems and so on. Confusingly, we had very different immediate backgrounds and upbringing.

In my late teens, I discovered a common thread in significant incidents that took place in the early to mid-twentieth century. My father, after fifteen years running Childrens' Homes and becoming a lecturer in social work, published a book: "A Place Called Hope: Caring for Children in Distress" (his catharsis). He told our family's story and his experiences as a residential social worker.

I discovered that my paternal grandparents had met in Northern France in 1918 where my grandfather had fought in the trenches in his late teens. My grandmother was a nurse. I cannot begin to imagine the horrors they witnessed.

At the end of the war they settled in the slums of Newport, South Wales, to unemployment, poverty and despair. Alcohol offered some relief while childbirth (including miscarriage, still-births, infant deaths) punctuated their ever bleaker lives.

In 1939, they were imprisoned for child neglect having been visited more than two hundred times by the National Society for the Prevention of Cruelty to Children (NSPCC). My father was already in an Approved School (youth prison) from the age of eleven (known as "Number Five", not by his name, Tommy). He was a beggar and a thief, the breadwinner of the family of about ten kids (who knew, who cared?) from the age of five. The family was split up and the three youngest brothers, taken into care.

Six years later, my Uncle Dennis, aged twelve, was dead.

He had been tortured, beaten and starved to death by foster parents. This became known as "The Story that took the War off the Front Pages" as, for months, it was national headline news. There was a Parliamentary Inquiry, a change in the law (the Children Act 1948), and, in an incredible twist, Agatha Christie based *The Mousetrap* on the events surrounding Dennis' death. It meant that my family was in the public eye with some disturbing consequences.

Even now, although I never knew Dennis, I feel like I can reach out to him – he feels so close.

Could this terrible tragedy have caused trauma sixty-five years later? Trans-generational trauma certainly explained the observed behaviours in my immediate family and gave me a rationale for my personal distress.

Reading my father's manuscript as an eighteen year old was, I remember, a moment of intense pride in what he had achieved but it was deeply disturbing to be exposed to the terrible events that had fragmented my family. My parents had never spoken about any of this to my brother, Bernard, and me and continued to avoid discussions about my Dad's childhood.

My psychiatrist, many years later, having read the book, told me that it had been the first time a client had his issues so clearly laid out in written form. "This will save a huge amount of analytical time."

I also discovered that poetry, both reading and writing, soothed my pain.

Medication, psychiatric treatment, psychotherapy and poetry enabled me to survive the terrible blackness of my depression. Eventually they would help alleviate and, possibly, overcome the effects of trauma.

I had planned, back in 1992, to compile a pamphlet of my poems that I felt might help people with depressive illness. In 2016, I found papers with my proposed title dated 7th August 1992: *Poems from the Unconscious: Reflections on Trauma, Recovery and Healing.* In the pile there were more than three hundred poems that I had written over those challenging years. It was fascinating to read these long-forgotten pieces, as well as discovering where I had written them. I found poems on pay-slips, boarding cards, meeting agendas, theatre tickets, faxes (remember them?) and most intriguing, on the back of a fixed penalty speeding endorsement.

Maybe there was something in me that drove me to write. I applied for an MA in Creative Writing at the University of Kent. I ended up studying for my MA, majoring in Poetry, in their fabulous facility in Montparnasse, Paris, near where I had lived forty years earlier. This was an opportunity to learn my craft and put it to good use.

In 2020, I was privileged to become a trained Samaritan volunteer. There are numerous calls from people suffering from depressive illness. The underfunding of social care has driven so many (too many!) sufferers to call mental health charities for help, including The Samaritans. The impact of Covid 19 has highlighted the flaws in the country's support structures. The Office for National Statistics has estimated a doubling of depressive illness during the pandemic in the UK from c10% to c20% of adults (Coronavirus and depression in adults, Great Britain: June 2020 ONS). That's more than ten million people!

In the last few years, I have been very open about my mental health issues as I believe that we all need to be aware of the number of people living with distress and the huge impact this has on society. The more we can reduce the stigma surrounding mental health the more supportive we will become. Jo eloquently expresses this in her foreword, for which I am grateful. She, and others, work so hard to reduce stigma and discrimination.

So now is the time to publish these poems from my unconscious and maybe, just maybe, help those who need, like I did, to escape from despair.

The Poems

In this book you will find traditional poetic forms such as blank verse, rhymed poetry, free verse, prose poetry, but also experimental poems (for example, "Childhood", a syllabic poem following the numerical sequence of the number π, and, partly inspired by e.e. cummings, "The Choice"). These were written over a period of thirty-five years, so styles vary. Some are very short (two words in one case) and the longest is a few pages. I invite you to either follow the narrative by reading them chronologically or you can dip in and out depending on your mood. You can see the subject of the poems through the titles and the brief introductory notes of each section.

The structure follows a narrative arc. **Transgenerational Trauma** is in two parts: the first part, *Origins of Trauma,* examines, through a series of prose poems, the trauma suffered by my paternal grandparents. I also describe the impact this had on my father and some of his siblings.

The second part, *The Ripple Effect*, contains poems that reveal the consequences of trauma on my generation and how we can recognise, endure and transform them.

Depression. These poems are personal musings written while I was in the depths of my worst moments. The rawness of the experience is echoed in the naïve, unstructured streams of internal monologue. I have left these as they were written at the time.

I wrote some poems in French (**Poèmes Français**) as this, I remember, helped me somehow to escape the reality of my pain. As I say in the introduction to these poems, "je peux me cacher à l'intérieur d'une langue étrangère" ("I can hide inside a foreign tongue"). I explore my relationship breakdown.

Suicide/Self-Harm/Survival reflects on those terrible moments when suicide and self-harm was a daily burden to survive. As I continued to write and work with my therapist, I managed to persevere with my recovery and then I could, somehow, start the healing process.

With **Healing**, I face full-on my blackness and actively seek the strength within the depression itself and make it a force for good. I could start to help myself, then others, to feel love again, a healthy love.

In **Solitude**, I recognise how poetry and art can reinforce healing. One can cope better even when bad things happen. Art is now.

Renaissance is where I find peace, familial love and humour.

Finally comes **The Beginning**. Blank pages for reflections by you, the reader.

Hopefully, through these poems, you can find solace or simply the joy, as I have, of reading poetry.

TRANS-GENERATIONAL TRAUMA

(TRANS-GENERATIONAL TRAUMA)

- There was an old woman
- Granddaughter "A lovely wealth"
- Family roots
- Father
- Grandfather
- Origins of Trauma
- Dad
- The Ripple Effect
- Three Blind Mice
- Children?
- Dennis speaks
- A tribute to Dennis
- Childhood
- Dance for Dennis
- Empathy
- Home
- Lament for Dennis

Trans-Generational Trauma

Trans-generational trauma theory was first developed in the 1960s in Canada when it was discovered that children of holocaust survivors were disproportionately referred for psychiatric treatment. Since then, it has been documented in the descendants of slaves, war veterans, refugees, survivors of interpersonal abuse, and many other groups. It's also particularly prevalent in victims of child abuse.

The thesis is that, not only can someone experience trauma, they can then pass the symptoms and behaviours of trauma on to their children, who then might further pass these along the family line. A ripple effect.

Childhood mistreatment can cause a cycle of abuse and anxiety in subsequent generations. Other situations that could cause trans-generational trauma include: extreme poverty, a crime against a family, a sudden or violent death of a close relative, a parent who fought in a war, torture of a family member.

These conditions were all present in my family.

Trauma can flare at any time.

Sufferers may find it harder to cope with life's stresses, get a good job, or be a good parent. They can have mental health problems, drug or alcohol issues, sex addiction, become involved in criminal activities, or show signs of harmful behaviour to themselves. Was this me? Would my children suffer the same consequences?

Origins of Trauma
Home

Inter-war Pillgwenlly, Pill, Newport. Docks, Slums. Welsh pirates' haven. Rows of blackened dockers' houses were lifeless. The coal, from the valleys, shipped to Empire, enriched merchants, entrapped poverty within stark, sunless dwellings. Narrow streets, an invisible maze, blocked all exits. The kids were shoeless, naked to cold, save for threadbare hand-me-downs. They huddled together with feisty anger.

John Thomas, "Jack", and Mabel Blodwyn, my grandparents, are on the merry-go-round. Night time flits, unpaid rent. Beatings, snuff, booze. Dirt.

Late night fumblings. Famished, filthily dirty kids asleep, while they conceive when the pub closes. Children are born. Frequently, inevitably.

National Society for the Prevention of Cruelty to Children visits more than two hundred times.

War breaks out again after twenty years of fug, brawls, drinks. Kids run away, imprisoned, removed. Two with foster father farmer Gough and wife. "March 1945, Jack and Mabel Blodwyn are at Goughs' trial. They see two of their sons Terence, Tommy. Dennis is dead."

Grandfather

Grandfather

Grandfather, I never met you. I can see you were good-looking with wavy blond hair. You look aristocratic in the photo. Army uniform with riding crop, 1916. Not so elegant in 1945, Gough's trial.

Although you are long gone, you are never mentioned except as a fighter and drinker, black sheep of our family of lawyers, entrepreneurs.

You grew up a street fighter. An Army boxing champion. You were a hard man. You wore a black hat which made you even harder. I know you used to beat my Nana, my Dad.

You joined the army in your teens for the First World War. In the trenches, you were brave fighting for the British, the enemy. Rejected by your family. Neglected. Disposable.

You were twenty two years old, she was twenty one. Mabel Blodwyn, from the Rhondda Valley, a nurse, on leave. You married in 1919 in Newport. You were a drunk. She was to become one. Embracing poverty, she lay with you, with love.

1923, abandoned in Newport, traumatised, unemployed, destitute, you are imprisoned for one month of hard labour for child neglect. Mabel Blodwyn seeks separation. She has ten, eleven more pregnancies with you. Eight survive.

Things became even more difficult for you after the birth of Dennis and Terence. The sixth and the seventh, probably. There was one bright spot, a letter from you to the NSPCC in 1935. It was full of good intention.

You wrote that you were sorry for the trouble you had caused after "all you have done for us. You will now see a great change. I am turning over a new leaf and am going to look after the home and the children, and I want you to have a word with the Missus. Let me know if there is anything I can do for you. I am a comic singer and can sing at any concert you arrange, or I can massage cripples."

December 1939, you, and this time, Mabel Blodwyn, imprisoned for child neglect, you cannot pay a fine of three pounds after two hundred and twenty two visits from the NSPCC. Farmer fined sixty pounds ten shillings for animal cruelty.

The children were taken or ran away.

Grandmother

Grandmother: "A Lovely Wreath"

There was an old woman of twenty-two, who will have so many children, she won't know what to do. Lost one runt already, she relieves her worn body of another. This one she wants to live.

Going without food days on end to feed the one or two before they became six seven more. Did you ever want to kill one? Nine in one room, kept them warm. Sores, scabs, drawers of unwashed clothes, undernourished.

Sniffing snuff, rubbing oily ointment to ease your aching, blind eye. Looking through the eye hole in the cell.

Another damning effect of childbirth, beatings. Weak muscles, tiredness, incompetence.

We came to see you. Don't touch anything, don't eat, drink. We won't stay long. Filthy, dirty, inescapable poverty.

Was it the poet tramp that took you to Pill? What is this life if full of care? All childhoods are normal to children who live them.

You didn't know where your children were until the trial. Your photo appeared on the front pages, the elegant clothes failing to hide your ignorance. At the Inquiry into Dennis' death, you thanked the council for the "lovely wreath" on Dennis' grave.

Do you remember how many children you had? I think I have met them all, apart from one.

Thomas John, Tommy, main breadwinner of the family. Street beggar at five years old. Burglar, thief. Caught stealing food, drink at eleven years old (or thirteen, who can be sure?). Taken to an Approved School, handcuffed in Black Maria. No longer Tommy just "number five". He was to become my father.

The NSPCC came to take the six remaining kids away. Betty, the eldest, escaped and looked after you until you died.

Dennis will die before his thirteenth birthday, on the 9th of January 1945. Tommy's birthday. Killed by his foster father. You had not seen him since November 1939. You attended the trial of the killer in your spanking clothes, paid for by the tabloid press. "Don't worry, they won't stay long".

Terry was on the straw paillasse freezing with Dennis when he died. The scars on his back have healed.

THE DAILY MIRROR

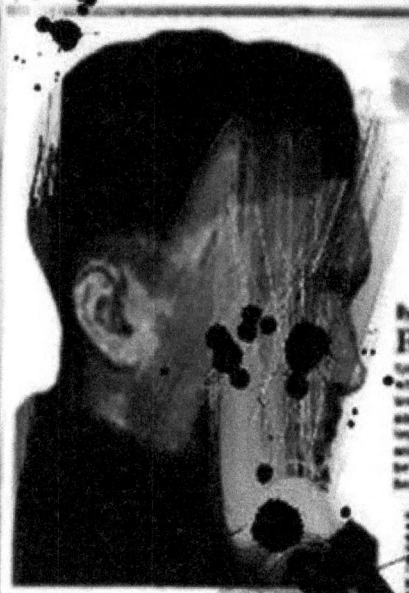

THE BULLY OF

His cold cruelty took a boy's life

By Your Special Correspondent

AFTER HIS FLOGGINGS HE READ PRAYERS

British soldiers wed Russians, speak by signs

The bed where Dennis died

P.C. Euphemia (5ft. 1in.) grabbed him

DUNLOP

KILLED DYING WIFE ON

ANK FARM | **This was his home**

A picture of the Gougher kitchen at Bank Farm. The cup-board on the left with the open door is the one in which Joseph O'Dohl was shot when shot up as a gentleman.

nce awaits fifth home | **Backing for land girls** | **30 gave him blood** | 'WE'LL KEEP OUR

Parson went by ... school of life

Bank Farm, Hope Valley, Shropshire

Scantily clad rash-covered children indescribable conditions Dennis and Terry end at Reginald Gough's Bank Farm Hope Valley the numbing boredom of evil anaesthetises kills compassion

struggle hope hold me with indifferent fingers his welfare we were all responsible wicked unholy fools Gough locked his wife in a stall with a savage bull escaping over the rafters gun threatened fear is my weapon of choice bounced head several times tiled-floor farm kitchen

she was dirty repulsive council visitor report lost caught in paper clip of another report blundering bungling plodders the barbaric philistine perseveres psychologists hold the view that if someone had thrashed Gough once early in his life it might have saved him your Behaviour has Shocked the World

Dennis O'Neill sucked on cow's teats ate raw swede unmercifully beaten slowly beaten with stick one hundred stripes a night straw paillasse on floor thrashed shivering stilled wind silenced by snow burdened conifers chill-blained cracked on back with stick struck violent blows on chest in December 1944 he did not attend school church fat-swathed in blunt worn worship soul as naïve as the sky I saw nothing to suggest he was not being properly cared for he cannot occupy a bigger smaller space he is neglected in such a manner as to cause serious injury to his health

slumbering dunces do not listen to the baggy sagging ones locked in a cubby hole legs blue and swollen stomach empty neglected his heart failed killed partly by slow partly by swift means in a shocking condition lying dead on a bed.

From this real life happening I took the idea for the Mousetrap — Agatha Christie

Sunday Mirror

1945-1966 and still the children suffer

HAD Dennis O'Neill lived he would now have been thirty-three years of age.

In fact, he died in 1945, a boy who never had a chance, shockingly and fatally ill-treated in a lonely Shropshire farmhouse.

Why, more than two decades later, do the Sunday Mirror recall this forgotten tragedy?

Because Dennis O'Neill was a foster child—a boy who, with his younger brother, was placed in the care of a local authority.

Shocked

The suffering of the O'Neill brothers, exposed by the courts and the national Press, so shocked the British people that the Government was forced to open an investigation.

The result was a new law promising greater protection for boys like Dennis.

Now the nation has again had its conscience stirred about the sufferings of a child "in care."

And it may well be that the law should be changed again. On Wednesday, this week, Home Secretary Roy Jenkins is to question the Chairman of the Dorset Children's Committee, Pamela Lady Digby, about the case of a boy now twelve years old who was repeatedly and viciously sexually assaulted by a youth while in the care of foster parents.

Again, it was only when the tragedy had reached the stage of a court case and a campaign led by the Sunday Mirror, that the story came out.

Mr. Jenkins has many vital questions to put to Pamela Lady Digby.

He must ask why the full details of the case were kept from the Dorset Children's Committee.

Why Pamela Lady Digby, her deputy and the children's officer, who knew something of what had happened, never even attempted to get all the facts.

Why the assaults were not discovered by the children's visitors.

How the foster mother failed to realise what was going on in her own home.

But even when these questions have been answered there is another which Mr. Jenkins must ask himself.

Is this outrageous case perhaps just a fringe of an unknown web of childhood misery?

Welfare

If he is in any doubt at all Mr. Jenkins must order a full and searching investigation into the welfare of children the nation takes into its protection.

In 1945, the system failed to save 13-year-old Dennis O'Neill.

In 1966 it did not help a boy of twelve.

There must be no more child martyrs.

Three Blind Mice

Three Blind Mice
Three Blind Mice
See how they run
See how they run

They run away from farmer and wife
Who cut off their tales with a carving knife
Then beat, tortured and starved them to death.
Three Blind Mice.

Agatha Christie wrote a radio play in 1947 to celebrate the 80th birthday of Queen Mary. She called it Three Blind Mice. This became The Mousetrap when it was produced as a stage play a few years later. She based this on the events surrounding the death of Dennis O'Neill in 1945.

With thanks to the Christie Archive Trust for the facsimile of the Sunday Mirror annotated by Agatha Christie

Where Are the Children?

The children are waiting the child itself is overlooked his pitiful life bolts free down corridors with crippling fear people of this country feel profound disquiet over the life and death of boy no fear for the pagan feast no repetition of these direful events voices of little children seem to be unnoticed system should be made to fit child not child to system

Members of Parliament were haunted yesterday ghost of Dennis O'Neill killed by farmer Gough memory of waif haunts the British people broken heart was kidnapped by a dream he was a child of the state

very proper widespread indignation tragic circumstances went wrong how to avoid the war inadequate staff makes me anxious silent failing cries unwanted children longing for affection they will never know

drink through dirty snot-encrusted blocked straws gripped in frozen nail-biting mouth wanton wastage of human lives parents still go on beating and bruising their children in their own homes crying in a darkened room boy found in a dark cellar with his hands tied behind his back.

no awareness of the state of misery bewilderment mother left them under a hedge denied the relief of her milk cheap whisky slow-mixed starves the famished chloroforms the spirit they slept in old broken black cots with the sides tied up with cords the mattresses fouled stained the antithesis of home children forced to live with senile adults in piss soaked clothes mental deficient cripples lacking the safety stimulus of parental love cold formality horrifying mental cruelty their souls become shrivelled

treat each child as a friend not a number don't kill the children imprisoned in shawls stay and hear my story bless the accursed blighted need every person of good will to be constantly on the watch one hundred and twenty five thousand children in institutions vast volume dull monotonous misery.

Betty

Betty, I am in Paris now, thinking of you. Your stained-yellow hair, crimson-cracked lips, loud Welsh slurring, slipping me an under-age drink. Beery, smoky laughter, alcohol-dimmed eyes hiding your effervescence, sadness.

Thick-powdered worn face, drawn by futile conversations, empty rooms. The bar props you up. I know you are no longer here, yet you outlived them all. You were always "larger than life," so maybe just maybe.

You thought it was the French sailor. It could not have been the Polish steelworker, that would be much later in better times. You found it difficult to remember them all. There were too many on the streets of Pill, Newport's dock slums.

Your baby's dad was one of the more exotic ones off the ships, who paid in strange currencies that you could change with the money lenders, buy a radio from the upstairs backroom, stockings from the cupboard under the stairs, even some Jamaican rum when you'd had a few good days.

Your Yvonne was a beauty. Why couldn't people see that? She died so young, about thirteen to fifteen months old.

Betty, how could anyone be sure after all this time? At last you lie in peace, together in Newport cemetery with your beloved Toni not far from your brother Dennis. You still remember the yells from the neighbours on the streets of Pill: "Black Bastard."

Tom O'Neill says: "The sufferings of my Brothers at the "Gough" farm, only make me more determined to tell of the Love of Christ."

Dad

On the grimy, unfriendly streets of Pill. In your patched-up rags, council issue stamped shoes, step-shorned head. Beggar at five dressed as Guy Fawkes, singing to tourists, pitying face outside bakers, looking after the rare car. Money to Jack who beat you. No school. How did you read the dictionary every day, the complete works of Shakespeare?

Progressed to thief, ringleader, Master Criminal. Hooking meat from the butcher's below the balcony in the indoor market, stealing sandwiches (value three shillings) to feed the family, friends. Arrested one month before your parents were imprisoned, family breakup, siblings in care. You, Approved School, taken away with your scabs, rash, unhealed wounds.

You found faith in the Salvation Army hostel where you were on your seventeenth birthday, the 9th of January 1945, when Dennis died. "The sufferings of my Brothers at the "Gough" farm, only make me more determined to tell of the love of Christ." Is that how you survived? What happened when you lost your faith?

Do you remember when you cried because I had run away and we hugged each other?

I am no longer afraid of the sad soliloquies of the evangelical social workers that could fill the Albert Hall, couldn't fill the hole in my heart, can't save the abused children how many names can I reel off from dear Dennis to Maria to Victoria to just the initialised P...

Faith Lost

Hope Valley, Shropshire, January 9th, 1948.

On the hill above
Hope Valley.
Facing the oak-stumps.
Blundering inoffensive fool
Cut them down.
They have re-grown.
Not you.
Wicked unholy fool
Cut you down.

Sat in solitude on
Forlorn oak bench.
Stilled and silenced
By snow burdened conifers.
On this most monstrous of days,
Now
On my birthday and your
Death-day.

I cannot pray
For you
Anymore.
I will always
Love you.

The boy's suffering threw light on 125,000 cases

UNWANTED CHILDREN SCANDAL:
THE FULL FACTS

Ill-treated, neglected ... on an index

By MONTAGUE SMITH

A scandal of modern times, the martyrdom ... conditions of Britain's unwanted children ... is told today by the Care of Children Committee, ... result of the manslaughter of Dennis O'Neill ... foster parents' farm in Shropshire.

The committee visited all kinds of institutions housing nearly ... children "mentally deprived" ...

... that the days of Oliver ... On the contrary, cruelties ... in every class of accommodation ... the reception of young children ... their homes to the time when, ... broken to spirit, they are sent ... world in which they have no friends.

Strachey: Why we stay on rations

'Must have more food than 1939'

MR. STRACHEY, the Food Minister, last night hinted that before he could introduce any drastic Elizabeth, will not, after all, sail this week for her maiden luxury voyage today.

No easy task

QUEEN E CHIEF'S ILLNESS

Sir Percy Bates will not sail

SIR PERCY BATES, chairman of the Cunard White Star Line, by Percy has been making preparations ...

Nuremberg Nazis hanged in pairs

GORING AND RIBBENTROP DIE FIRST

From Daily Mail Special Correspondent
NUREMBERG, Wednesday Morning.

AT a minute past midnight the executions began of the 11 Nazi leaders condemned to death by the Allied Tribunal. Two gallows were used: Goring and Ribbentrop were the first to die. Then, in twos, followed Kaltenbrunner, Keitel, Rosenberg, Frank, Frick, Streicher, Sauckel, Jodl, and Seyss-Inquart.

Early last night security officers were posted at each entrance to Nuremberg's grim, red-stone gaol to guard against attempts by fanatical Germans to stage any demonstration.

The bodies will be interred in an unidentified plot of ground. The authorities, remembering how Mussolini's grave was defiled, do not want a repetition here.

Bon Marche chief is found dead

MAGNETIC MINE KILLS EIGHT

ZAGREB DEATH PLEA REJECTED

Loved a German, died on line

Heath dies today

Cupboard Love!

2 YEARS IN ARMY FOR ALL

Then four with Territorials

By Daily Mail Political Correspondent

'L' DRIVER TESTS TO BE HARDER

'Chattels' pay next April

Dartmoor's soldiers

FOSTER PARENTS ACCUSED OF MANSLAUGHTER

Boy killed by cruelty, prosecution says

HANDCLASP in a Crimean garden

Two courts criticise two Government departments
Attempts to usurp our powers

Express Staff Reporter

THRASHED UNTIL STICK BROKE

PONTESBURY, Shrewsbury, Monday.

THE life and death of 13-year-old Dennis O'Neill at a lonely farm in Shropshire was described at Pontesbury, Shrewsbury, today, when his foster father and mother were accused of the boy's manslaughter.

The foster parents were Reginald Gough, 31-year-old farmer of Bank Farm, Hope Valley, Minsterley, Salop, and his wife Esther, aged 29.

EYES RIGHT—AND HAIR RIGHT

BABY'S BOTTLE MURDER ALLEGED

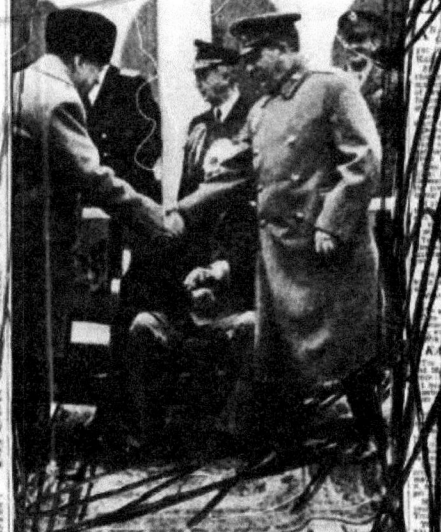

Dead on bed

A Tribute to Dennis

The plays the thing that made the name
Agatha Christie's The Mousetrap.
It was your story.
Seven million people have seen Terry avenge you.

Queen Mary celebrated her birthday
listening to his revenge
with two million others.

Your brothers will reach out to
more than fifty thousand.
My poems may reach a few.

Parliament debated, changed the law.
Some children were saved, many will be saved.
The Nazis surrendered the Front Pages.

Stalin avoided Churchill's, Roosevelt's eye
stretched out to read your story.
Was your death tragedy or statistic?
You were not a Jew, nor one of the
Former People,
writer, poet, artist.
Just a poor boy.

Gough's lawyer protested
"This is British
Not German justice."
As Ribbentrop, Streicher
swing,
The unwanted children
lay inert, waiting death
in their thousands
across their dark world.
Your killer could not make
Eichmann's plea.

*Let's hear your brother Terry,
who was with you when you died,
speak:
"I wanted to be better
than the perpetrators, no I do not seek revenge"
He even loved the way Agatha Christie
dramatised The Moustrap, how she imagined
he would feel, turning him
into a vengeful,
schizophrenic, homicidal, sex maniac.*

"Fantastic" said my beautiful, sweet Terry.

The Ripple Effect

There Was an Old Woman

Once upon a time
This mother
Lost
(yet another)
Child
She lost her mind

No time to care

Soon
She would belch out another
from a too fertile womb

This child
Lost
His mother

This child
Picked up
The pieces
there   *are*
There they are
no   On the ground
Strewn around   *words*
His children's feet.
to
describe   *the pain*

Childhood

Begone, moronic mush from his face.
Bewildered
smile, petrified mouth. Cautious, hidden eyes.

Cries,
silent, failing,
to
displace fear. Born an
orphan quick-buried in ragged shawl.
Denied
relief of Mother's milk.

Lost in darkened room,
his dry mouth
howls with pleasure on
Christmas Day, no fear for the pagan
feast, no consoling milk. Protected,
imprisoned wrapped in the shawl.
Later, in wee-soaked trousers, blue eyes
still shine through,
distress
deep in face.

He bolts free down corridors with
a crippling fear,
Cloaked, bound within the shawl.
Peeeeing
the highest, show willy,
save face, killing

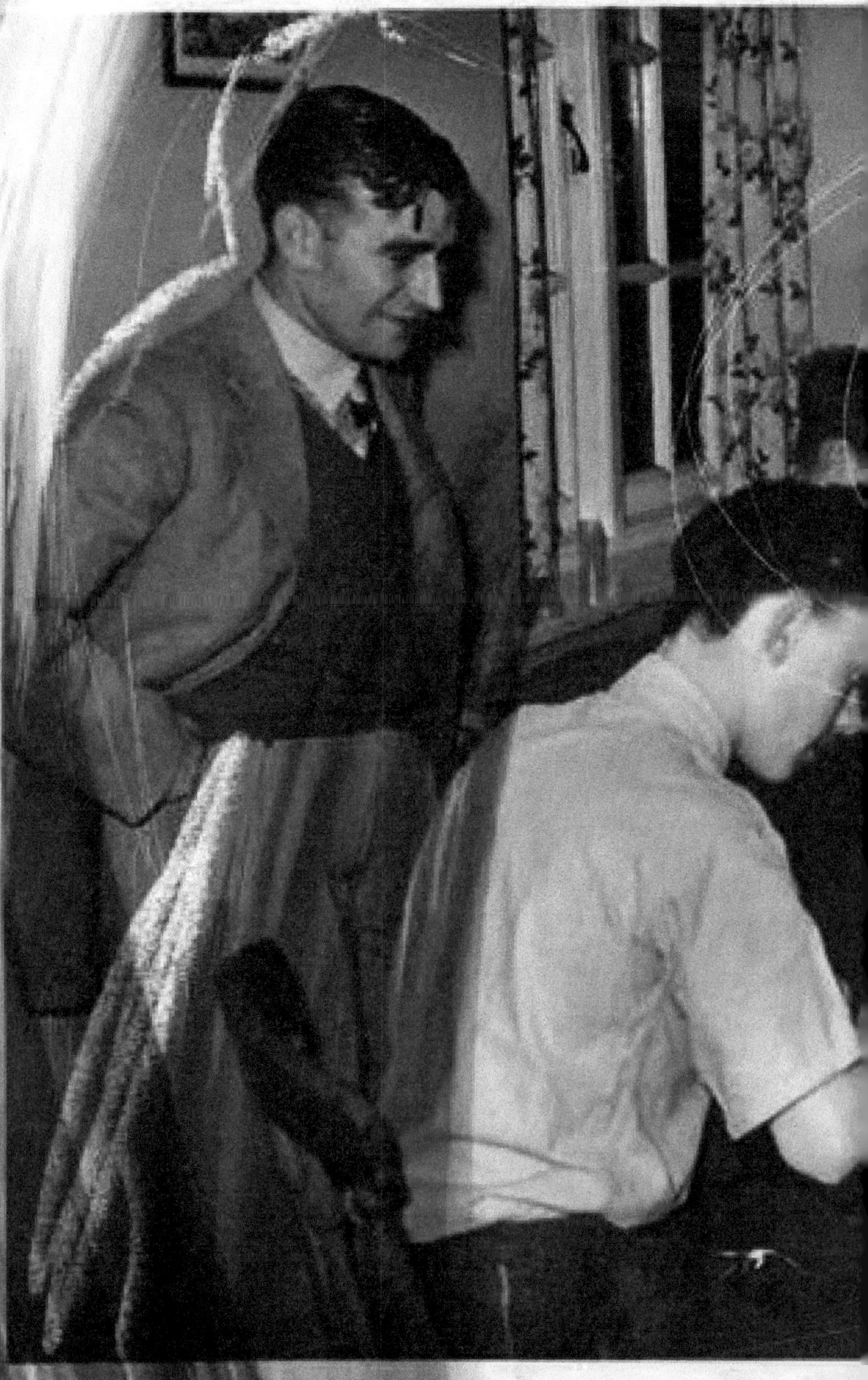

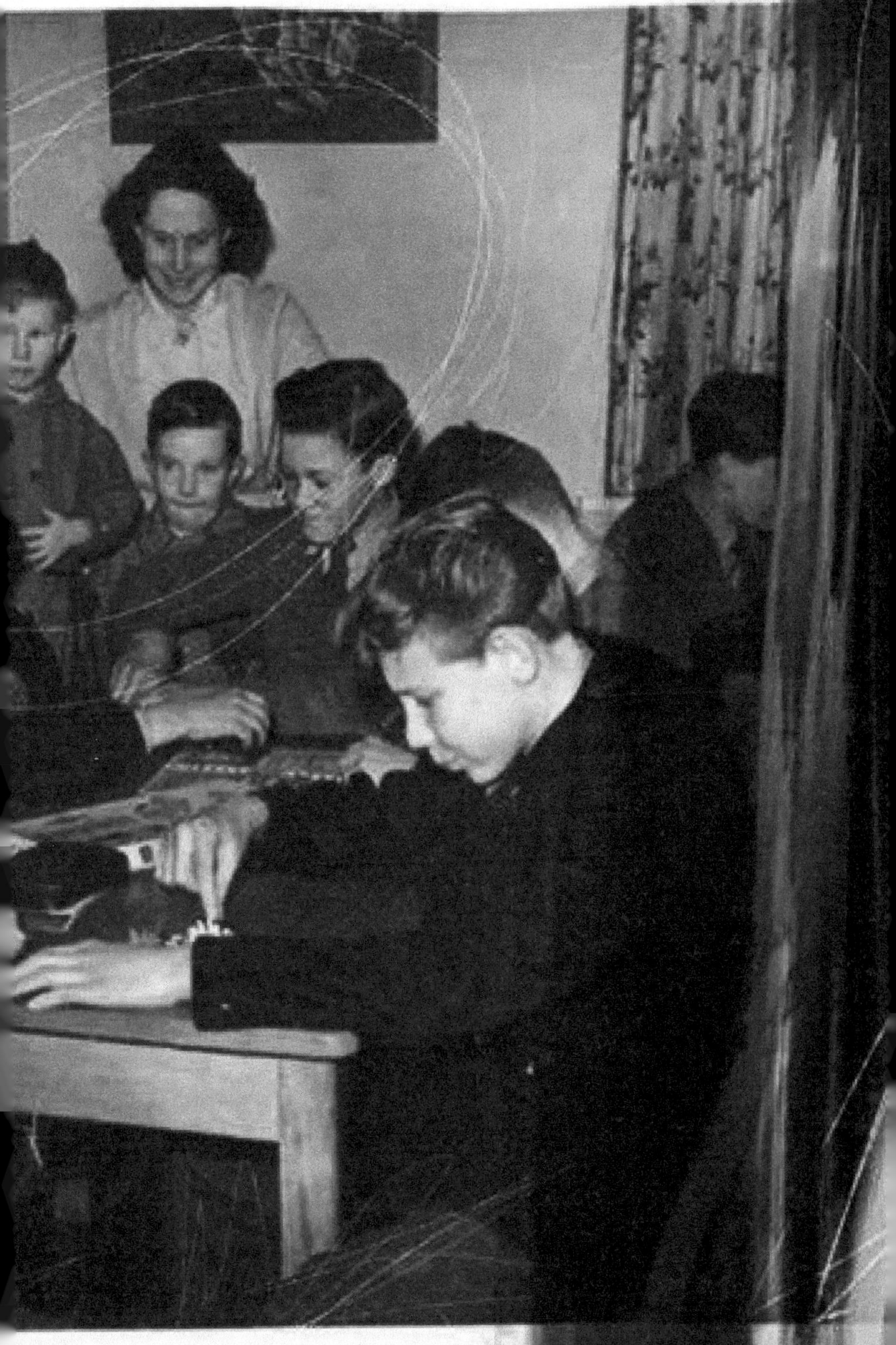

spiders and
flies. With sniper's eyes throw stones at
mites who dance
with tea-milk,
bloated,
billowing Miss Freebody
whose mouth is a gaping gob stuffed
with digestives. His shawl

fetters him
to her messed up carcass. Black eyes
blinded by sticking tape, mouth scarred.
Sniff girls' knickers,
bras,
inhaling milk. Breathe deep comforts, sex
etched his defiled face. Let them
Fall. To punish kills the fear.

Let them fall, watched by no-colour eyes
seeing few
promises. Chemical breast milk starves
the famished, yet chloroforms the fear.
A brief moment
of respite before yearning
for the lost refrain.

Drink cheap whisky slow
– mixed with powdered milk makes Christmas
sleep pure.

Wake up with drawn face. Drink dirty milk,
snot-encrusted glass, blocked straws
gripped in frozen,
nail-biting mouth. Sleeping, living, dreams
of white-faced fear
since the first strained cry.
Those childhood eyes full of cold despair,
mouth sucks
the shawl dry

of fear. Promised warm comfort
from the arms of future lovers.
Future
Hope. No milk, childhood: none.
Childhood begone.

Dennis Speaks

My body stumbling
in cow-dung sodden spinney.
Furrow trudging,
falling into ice-filled troughs, splashing
a splash that drenches
lawmakers, dramatists, criminals,
social workers, poets, family,
You?
The lakeshore breaks, locks, dams,
levées lose moorings
tears raise the swell
amplify angry lunatic tides,
magnificent waves sweep…

It happened to Christ. Pilate.
It will come to
The Wandering Jew. We all die.

This is how it starts:
the heart stops,
blood flow ceases, pools form
royal, virgin colours paint the skin,
less cold than outside but cold sets in
stiff as a stick I cannot escape
my eyelids freeze on a banal gaze
I cannot feel any kind touch
from the carry man
who feels my heart-breaking twitch
that is a natural death.

my bowels are empty already
advanced putrefaction prepares well my body
black scabs of wool adhered to neglected feet
cracked, chapped heels
too long toe nails grow no more
no sub-cutaneous fat.
the moaning is done the eyes bulged tongue swelled.

That may have been the end of it
And you who watch and read and listen to this story
Better for you, and me, to pass on
Change time
Change the world
Light without a shadow

Lament for Dennis

This *fait divers* of your death
Not fully mourned
swamped my heart
claimed my hurt
shaped this verse

For the children who follow.

I'd never cried with despair locked in the cubby hole or tied to the pig bench or washing naked in freezing troughs waiting my one hundred strokes or more with Terry exchanging enforced blows because the farmer foster father was tired and then tired no more

bludgeoned them another one hundred so here I am with my family counting not the blows but the unmistaken scars of those events of so long ago that dragged us into alcohol drugs sex money I will drag us out again become the great healer so stay and hear my story and bless the accursed blighted children

It took me thirty years
to realise I will live
survive them throwing me in with the demented
psychopaths, deviants,
freezing wet nights
I abused my body.
You.
Now I can smile and make you laugh
and bury the ghost of my dead Uncle.

"fait divers" is a minor news item

DEPRESSION

- Combo
- it really hurts
- Plea[se]
- How close?
- dying is hard to ignore the mirror on my back
- TEARS
- a long time ago
- if only
- gallery
- Thanks
- of abuse
- ten years
- The Black hole

Depression

As I attempt to offer succour to sufferers through my poetry, I also ask others to show them empathy and respect.

Why respect? What many people may consider to be minor events can create a surge of despondency and despair in the ones experiencing them. There may be a deeper cause.

The worst feelings I had were when I couldn't control or stop the dramatic effects of my depression on my daily life even though I could sense the onslaught of those black moments.

Comb

I had just stepped out of the shower.
I noticed, before combing my hair,
one plastic tooth, eager to sever
from its shared shaft, to lie alone, bare.
Then, irreversibly, it did.
I am not materialistic, vain.
I often comb my hair with my fingers.
I didn't, ever, anticipate a comb's tooth
F
      A
           L
                L
                    I
                        N
                            G

I was engulfed by a Tsunami of sadness.

How Close?

Smash the egg
Crack the wing
Break it
Rip the beak

Slit-slice the skin
Tear the tendon
Take it
Crush the feet
Sear the hair
Burn the eyes
Stake it
Stamp the beast

Spill the rules
Kill the fools

Forsake it
What fucking
rules?

A Long Time Ago

Woman
in a darkened room,
no door
no movement

I had more movement in the womb.

Floundering on
shabby slab
gashing gasping
for air
which kills me.

Need feed,
suckling nipples

but that was a long time ago.

Gallery

Blood red off
coarse canvas
spills onto the translucent walls
by the sly eyes that nobody
sees
seas of blood
guts
with upturned blistering
stained
corners.

Plea

Give me your love
Now
Believe me I will die
Without your love
Now

If Only

we could be together
we wouldn't
we wouldn't be together
we would
be.

Solitude

Here now
in solitude
I will not say
I love you
as surely
it will end

TEARS

WORDS THAT DRIP FROM THE PEN
WET THE PAGE
THAT'S WHY I WRITE WITH A PENCIL
WHICH IS WHY YOU CAN READ
THESE WORDS.

Tears

Words that drip from the pen
wet the page
that's why I write with a pencil
which is why you can read
these words.

Ten Years

Decade
Decayed.

The Black Horse

Roaring soaring
Scuffling clawing
Slicing pouring grief
the black black horse
Turning squirming
Retching burning
Crying dying
So scared
So pregnant with fear
So controlling

It Really Hurts

I have never known so much pain,
It's there but I can't see the cause
Or can't accept the cause.
Why do I feel the pain?
When it's not true what's happening to me?
I can't accept
But want the pain,
Because then somehow it will go away
But it doesn't.
The tears no longer offer relief.
Does the sea really wear away the cliff?
I pray that it does,
Although I cannot see it
Why is it there like a boulder,
Taking an invisible eternity to leave me?

Why doesn't she love me?
Why can't I rid myself of the hurt?
Where is the time that heals?
When will I ever be better?

When will I find my core?
My seed to grow?
Somewhere I have the strength,
The vision to see the end
Oh My God, please let it come soon.

Thanks

i don't want to disturb
the balance of society.
is that why I'm disturbed?
is that why I'm unbalanced?

Self Abuse

Fear smears,
`tis not noble.
pain wanes,
does not grow.
fate hates,
not disallows.
only love can seal the vows.

Sorrow borrows
only time.
heartbreak faked
will destroy
forsaken ache
with sodden will
stretched, scorned love will quick, then still.

Trying so Hard to Ignore the Chimera* on My Back

i can lay blind inside the calm mother. i can smack the world. i can cry, i can suck the dried cracked nipples. i can feed on the whisky-diluted milk. i can plead for the mothers not to kill themselves. i can avoid learning how to speak, walk. i can warm myself in the urine-soaked bedding.

i can snuggle against the old hag's armpits. i can dream of future smelly sex. i can anticipate the comfort of tender love. i can reflux the mourning. i can eat. i can drink. i can live.

i can lie stretched on the harsh table. i can be three years old. i can feel the fingers touching playing probing. i can see the girl. i can see she is twelve years old. i can not see the adults.

i can feel the irresistible urging of the chimera deep claw-stuck-fast on my back nudging me inexorably to the front of this deathly procession.

i can swear i can throw stones at the bloated carcass of the digestive munching teacher. i can untie my hairclip. i can be a scholar.

i can smell the sweat of too close numb-skulls. i can see the knickers of the old ladies. i can grasp the knickers off the line. i can smell them. i can be beaten for that. i can weep when Mother, calm, can smack, not hug, me. Yet

i can feel the irresistible urging of the chimera deep claw-stuck-fast on my back nudging me inexorably to the front of this deathly procession.

After Baudelaire

i can believe the ads. i can be good at school i can be bad at school. i can hurl swear words with intellectual curiosity from the corner. i can still refuse to eat. i can be quite brilliant. i can master chess. i can fail exams i can fail brilliantly. i can write a bit. i can paint. i can talk incessantly. i can read well. i can write. je peux me cacher à l'intérieure d'une langue étrangère. i can talk a lot. i can masturbate. i can write well i can give nothing. i can give a jot. i can give a lot.

i can feel the irresistible urging of the chimera deep claw-stuck-fast on my back nudging me inexorably to the front of this deathly procession.

i can have sex with milk bottles, shampoo bottles, pillows, legs. i can have sex with fruit, sand sculptures. i can have sex with all women, any age, any nationality, all colours, all sizes , shapes, smells, looks, intelligences. i can gnaw, strike, fight flesh. i can quit quickly the tossed bed. i can hide in folds of quilted luck.

i can love her. she can love me. i can make love with her before she dies. i can leave her. she can take her own life.

i can feel the irresistible urging of the chimera deep claw-stuck-fast on my back nudging me inexorably to the front of this deathly procession.

i can reach old age. i can be confused by dates, events, lost.

i can fall drunk. i can make love with too old too young too many. i can ask if there is another one to come.

i can feel the irresistible urging of the chimera deep claw-stuck-fast on my back nudging me inexorably to the front of this deathly procession.

i can think about death. i cannot rehearse death. i cannot learn death. i cannot buy one hundred years. i cannot be immortal. i can love stay calm and death won't give a damn.

i can dampen the sound. i can shut out the light. i can realise that old age ain't wisdom. i can go mad with hunger. love is now dead.

i can do anything to feel alive.

yet i can still feel the irresistible urging of the chimera deep claw-stuck-fast on my back nudging me inexorably to the front of this deathly procession.

Poèmes français

(Compréhension
la vie fade
Amour Deedu
Tu es là)

Poèmes Français 1992   French Poems 1992

I wrote these poems in French. I believe it enabled me to hide my pain somehow by writing in a foreign language. I enjoyed the wordplay as well. This is my first attempt to translate them after thirty years. If you can, enjoy them in French first.

Je peux me cacher à l'intérieure d'une langue étrangère.

I can hide inside a foreign tongue.

Compréhension	**Understanding**
Si un jour	If one day
tu comprendras	you will understand
que t'aimerai toujours	I will love you forever,
sans remords	no remorse,
tu respecteras	you will respect
notre esprit et corps	our spirit and body.
si un jour	If one day
je comprendrais	I would understand
que tu m'aimais	that you loved me
sans regrèt	without regrets,
je respecterais	I would respect
ton désir de paix	your wish for peace.
si un jour	If one day
nous comprendrons	we understand
que nous nous aimons	that we loved each other
sans tristesse	without sadness,
nous respecterons	we will respect
notre sagesse.	our wisdom.

La Vie Fade

Je ne veille plus à l'amour
qui vieilli
je ne me réveille plus
l'amour ne se réveillera plus

je ne veille plus à la boule noir

qui m'envahit
je laisse le cheval noir
je me lasse du cheval noir

l'amour noircit
la passion devient la tendresse
devient la sagesse
de l'enfance
la naissance me noit
je respire la noyade
la vie fade
ne recommencera plus.

Dull Life

I will no longer watch over
love that ages.
I will not wake up
the love that no longer
wakes up.
I will no longer watch over
the black ball
that invades me.
I'll leave the black horse.
I'm weary of the black
horse.
Love blackens
passion becomes tenderness
becomes childhood
wisdom
birth drowns me
I breathe the drowning.
Dull life
will not return.

Amour Perdu

un clin d'amour
un brin d'amour
un bain d'amour
un grain de soleil
un bout de réveil
une envie de dormir
un rire d'envie
un chagrin dessus
un dessus de lit
un cri d'espèce
une espèce de fou
un fou d'espoir
un désespoir
un clin d'amour
déclin d'amour.

Lost Love

flicker of love
fibre of love
shower of love
flower of stars
sliver that stirs
need to sleep
needy laugh
gloom atop
top of a bed
animal scream
mad scream
mad hope
hopelessness
flicker of love
failure of love

Tu es là	**You are there**
Tu es quand même là	At least you are there
je suis donc heureux	so I am happy
de t'aimer	to love you
le jour ou tu mourras	the day you die
sera le jour	will be the day
de ma néance	of my nothingness
mon obéissance	my surrender
de la vie	to life
est totale	is total
que personne ne m'en veuille	no-one should blame me
je n'en veux pas	I don't want it
sauf à la négation	save the rejection
de l'amour	of love
je suis quand même	at least I'm still
heureux	happy
de t'aimer là.	To love you there.

SUICIDE
SELF-HARM
SURVIVAL

Suicide, Self-Harm, Survival

The names of some of my therapists in chronological order have been:

Grieves (psychiatrist), Edge, Blows, Welbe, Joy. I'm so glad it was in that order, after thirty years, I ended with Joy!

It's very important to find the right therapist. I was emotionally and sexually abused by one (female) therapist who I will not mention by name. "Therapist" is not even an anagram!

They all, with one obvious exception, contributed to my eventual well-being by listening, by hearing. So thanks.

I wrote a poem about my experience of contemplating ending my life. I was relieved that I had discovered a sense of happiness. My friends and family thought therefore that the danger of suicide had elapsed. No. I decided I wanted to kill myself because I was so scared of returning to that living hell of severe depression (something that non-sufferers don't get), partly because I wanted to "die happy." The saving response was: "but who's to say you will not be even happier in the future?" Thanks Polly Welbe.

I wonder how many of us would imagine that "happiness" itself, in someone with depression, can lead to suicidal thoughts?

Never forget to talk, to listen, to hear.

Mutual Understanding

If I could explain to you in a straightforward way

I wouldn't.

The Whole Circle

I know too much
Therefore I don't want to live with all the others.
I wish there was a western
Hari Kiri
That's what I want to do
Be respected for it:
By my children.
No depression,
No blackness,
But light,
The light of Hari Kiri.
Clean, pure
Beauty.
The ultimate choice.
Isn't it predictable, inevitable
It's got to be done
In the right way.

The Psychiatrist

Well, thanks for coming.

Yes it's been very difficult.

Well, he's smartened himself up today.

I'm hoping we can settle things here as I feel we can still make it. As a couple I mean.

He still hasn't accepted that we're no longer together. I'd like you to help him get it and move on. I'm really worried.

What about?

Well y'know he's been seeing you for a while and I know he has really suffered in the past with depression. You know more than me now but probably childhood trauma and I'm not equipped to deal with that but I am really worried he'll kill himself.

Yes I think that's a real possibility but that's not your responsibility and you have to move on for sure. You can't let him drag you down.

You agree he might kill himself!?

Yes but you mustn't think about it.

I am here, you know.

Yes see how pathetic he looks, not so smart now – a bit crumpled I would say.

Thanks.

Escape

Why would I not like to escape from this world?
(or can I believe in a better place?)

When I Was Sixty-Four

My fear
for old age
is the sorrowful
lack of decadence.

Dates confused,
events lost,
physical intimacy gone.

Imagine
falling drunk,
smacked by drugs,
making love with
too old,
too young,
too many.
Anything to feel alive.
Feel.

My only fear
for old age
is the sorrowful
lack of self-destruction.

A Meeting

Tend towards
but never meet
light upon a shadow

Wild dreams of hopelessness
caressed with soft
seas of sound
deluge of passion
awakes the thrusting senses

Life rhythms wrench
the reverie
of ill-acquired deceptions

Puff-hearted hopes
drag forth
dead-brained stuttering wit

the dull, wet comfort of childhood
is aborted
painful light meets light
cheek, tendertouches cheek
feel the smile
stay
live the real heartache

I Will Die Happy

Breathless, in my darkening room,
deadened floor, frozen walls.
Sun dulled by stained shutters.
Life choked, laughter stalls.
I want to die.

I soon learned how to hold you.
I felt your love-gift of joy.
I can return to happiness,
I can become that little boy.
I want to die happy.

I ran away from that cold, wet, place.
Finally happy, finally well,
I have love now. I will kill myself.
I cannot go back to hell.
I am dying, happy.

"Stay awhile," I hear you say,
You still have something to give.
Feel that healing, soothing tone.
Later, happier seasons to live.
I will die happy.

always well
Bernard

61

Money Talks

I disgusted you.
If only you had respected me.
You wasted me.
You lost me, tried to
shame me,
blame me,
for so many ills.
So much despair, lack of
self-esteem.
Lately, you used me to help in your
self-destruction.
I stayed inert and indifferent,
unavailable, unattainable, remote,
which changed
nothing
in your
distorted, dysfunctional world.
Yet now I am here for you
in one final effort to save your life;
what am I to you?

Addiction

I will live, I will survive. I will tell you how they burned my books, smacked me down, beat me up. Made me fat, made me ugly. Made me a drunk.

I was a genius, so proudly reading the bible to the congregation in the village Salvation Army Hall. I was a self-taught three year old prodigy.

The Rupert the Bear annual thrown on the fire – that should do it. The crushing of my precocious talent, the birth of my little brother? I'll never read his poems.

I'm fifteen years old, Dad telling me the story of his criminal past, his dishonesty destroyed me once more. I couldn't look at him for two years.

I wake up and grab the bottle of vodka by my bed. Take a quick slug to stop the cold sweats, trembling hands. Crisps spilled out onto the sofa. Lunch missed. I go to a different shop to pretend there is no pattern. The stick I use doesn't always work as I tumble over walls. Shaking hands disable texting for help. The carton of milk flows down my front. I won't spill the vodka. Lost bank card. Lost money. Lost. Car written off a long time ago. Dirty clothes, piss-stained or worse. Plates, cutlery, cups, glasses slammed in cupboards, drawers.

Seventy years on and it's no longer acceptable to die like this.

You drive me to Rehab.

I will not drink. I will die if I drink. I am surprised. The clinician is surprised I am alive. I survive. Five years dry. You, my little brother, saved me and bought me a Rupert the Bear annual from 1954. It's time to catch up on my reading. Maybe I will read your poems.

Now that I've saved you, can I please take care of myself?

Look after Yourself

One root I had
was my love for you.

It was dried, ripped. Yet it survives.

I still wait a water drop from you, a little tenderness.

It would become
the most beautiful, dangerous rose.

I would have offered to you
If you had stayed with me.

*In the event of a decompression,
an oxygen mask will automatically appear in front of
you.
If you are travelling with someone who requires
assistance, secure your mask on first,
then assist the other person.*

One root among many
was my love for you.

It was parched, torn.
Yet lives on.

I nurture it every day with devotion.

It has come of age,
a gentle, wild daisy,
I hold to my heart.

Catharsis

Lord Denham House of Lords 1945:

"It is my view that Mr. Gough, who has been sentenced to six years' penal servitude, would be very much better treated if, during the next six years, every quarter, or every six months, he could have ten or sixteen blows with the cat."

You look so relaxed waiting trial who gave you bail allowed you to sell the farm watching five hundred people from a bedroom window the dishevelled bed sold for five shillings not a bed a fetid urine blood-soaked paillasse where Dennis died Terry lives his nightly nightmares

Your stupid repulsive dirty wife chose prison to escape you the baying throng of too late ladies wrapped in their furs buying tickets bribing policemen ten pounds for the trial all the hotels are full

Is the cushion comfortable comforting do you think your haircut respectable are you reading about your exploits you'll make the front pages replace the war for a bit not quite comic relief are you warm in front of the stove

Warm enough to discard your coat in that grubby scullery where indifferent soup would stew gurgle that Dennis Terry never tasted did you nonchalantly throw your hat on the chair how did you light the cigarette did the photographer propose it to give you a confident insouciant air

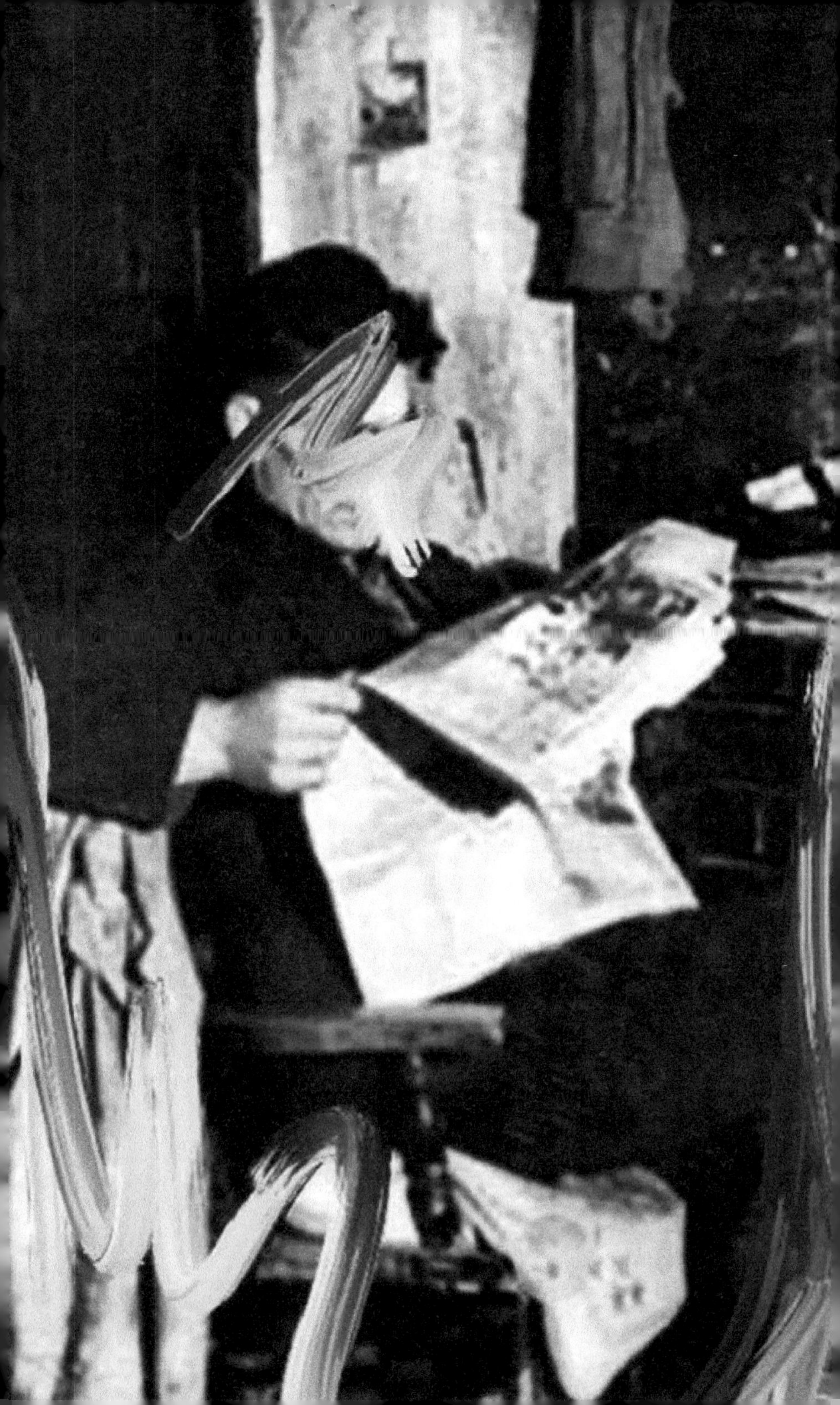

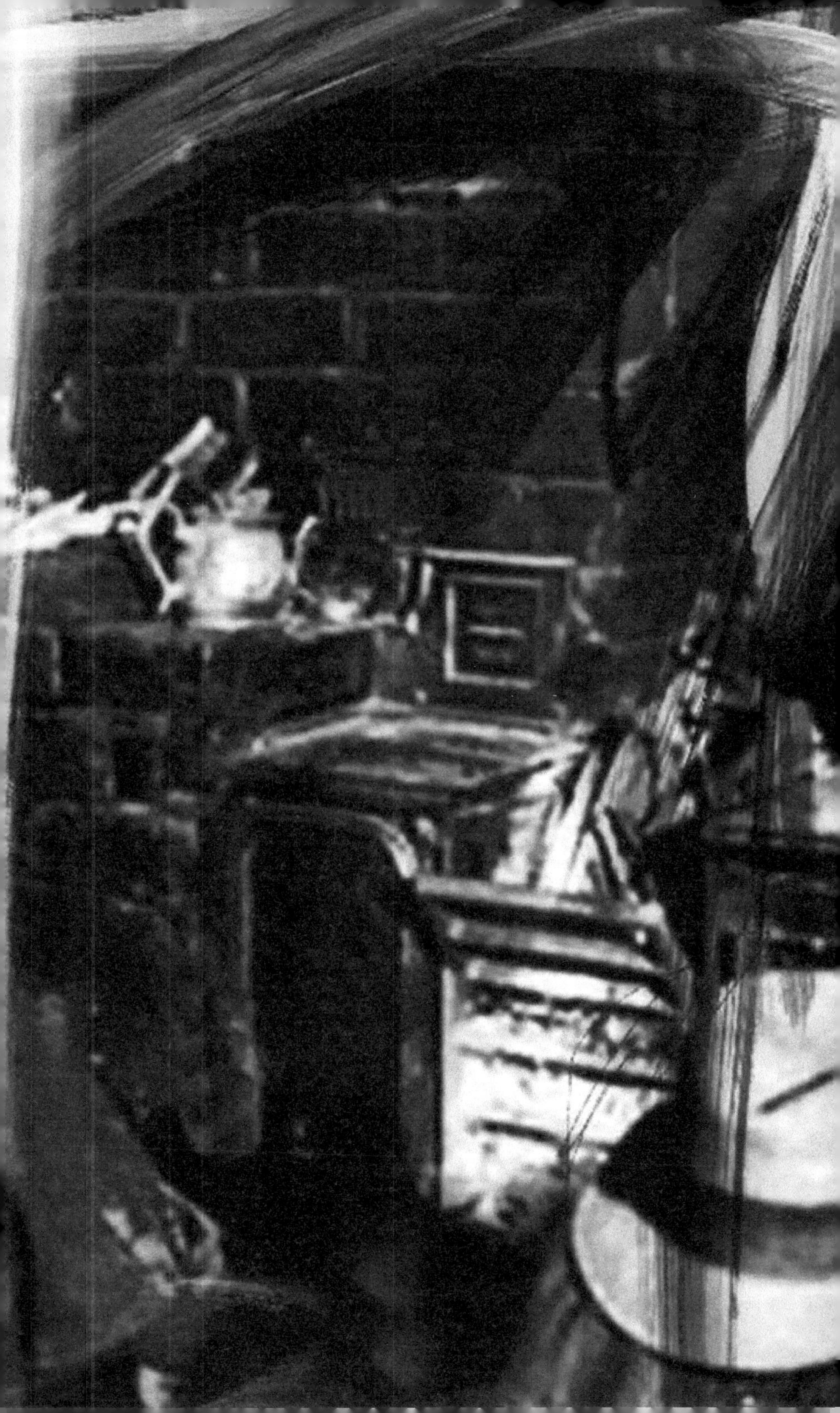

I can see your dirty trouser turn-ups do you think you can influence the outcome is that the airless black cubby hole six feet by three feet six inches by three feet six inches behind you where Dennis would be locked anticipating his beatings with a despairing acceptance simple tiredness of your pathetic brutality

Where is the pig bench that Dennis was tied to where you made them strike each other you were tired re-energised enough to strike them again where is the lamp so you could see their pain they are waiting for you in the court room the rope the sticks I don't care what you are thinking feeling I will tell you what will happen seventy years into the future. I will find you.

I have found you. I have counted
Every day you bludgeoned
Starved, tortured my family
Tied them to the pig-bench

I have been to Bank Farm
To Hope Valley
Found you in that befouled place
Dug up the dirt, scraped the walls

Smelled your stinking pestilence
Spat it all in that spiked kettle
Mixed with my piss shit
My gagged up vomit.

Sparked it with a clip of the sun
Tossed in some bloody broken sticks
Dead chicken's claw, cows' teats
Raw swede, horse's hair.

A cut up photo of you singed
A sliver of sharp ice
Broken from the trough
Where cows, horses drank

And naked children washed.
Sealed with burned earth
From an angel's grave
In a place you cannot access

There is no release
Even in Hell from this
Incremental, exponential torment
I have found for you

I have buried any hope
In the secret cubby hole
That contains the love that you
Can never reach.

HEALING

The divorce
Coping
Blade Ball
Greater love
Comfort
Discomfort
Poet
The Drunken Chugger
American Dreams
Deserving
Do Not Cry For Me
The Old lovers
The Scent Of you

Healing

Edith Eger, the renowned psychiatrist and Auschwitz survivor, in her book "The Choice", discusses healing, from her own terrifying experiences. She realises that she had buried her trauma (faced with danger, the option of fight or flee was not available in Auschwitz – she chose to "freeze"), and could not raise it with her children who in turn suffered trauma. "It's not just my own loss that hurts; it ripples out into the future." They had no grandparents (perished in the camps) but the children were not allowed to ask why their friends had grandparents but not them.

At some point, she realised that her experiences needed to be faced: "If there is one small piece of hell I miss, it is the part that made me understand that survival is a matter of interdependence, survival is not possible alone." She made the choice to speak about her time in the camp and, only then, could healing begin. "Running away doesn't heal pain; it makes it worse."

She was fortunate in that she had people who could listen to her. This made me think that just talking about trauma is only half the story. A "listener" who tells a depressed person to "get a grip" will surely not alleviate the anguish. In order to heal there must be a non-judgemental listener, possibly a Samaritan. An empathetic listener for those poor souls who finally have found the courage to speak about their trauma can save them as well as future generations. They will finally be heard.

I was finally heard.

The Choice

Li(f)e
Keep (war)m
Stay St(ill)
S(tiff)
Desp(air)
Sc(are)
Di(stress)
Petr(if)ication

i

W(or)ry

(sh)   y?

I
L(if)e
Streng(then)
Magn(if)y
Intens(if)y
Em(b(r(ace)
Beaut(if)y
It's y(our)
Coo(led)

cho(ice)

Choose Life

Coping

The lines between show the
sad face
short sorrow turns the furrow
tomorrow
life's labour will smack
the tilled smile back

Black Ball

The sharp cutter spoon
Scoop
with ice-white hard beats
the rank black balls
from the guts spill out
down the gallery walls.

Oh sharp cutter spoon
Cut,
Cut deep and quick,
the furry fury glues
from the soul out
of the heart's sodden fuse.

Now sharp cutter spoon
Lift
with ease and grace
that bastard evil puss
from the hidden holeout
so that I can be us.

Greatest Love

The make-up falls
from her face
dull-eyed tears smear
as they drip-drop onto
the parched note
this love is now done
better love the next one.

Poet

I am a poet
because
I cannot be anything else.
I am a poet
because
I can be everything else.
I am a poet
because
I can be.
I am a poet
because
I am.

Comfort

The Wheel of Fortune chokes
spokes grounded in
comfort's quagmire.

Comfort dissipated by discomfort
thus formed
Fortune's Wheel, then allows
its cycle once more to rouse.

Discomfort

This chair
ain't big enough
for the both of us.

American Dreams

As a child, I ran wild with my white cord,
braided, tucking a many-coloured tea
towel over drooping woollen swim shorts
that coldly cling above moccasined feet,

swiped out of Bopa's kitchen with the hand-
held knife ready for battle; kill me or
be killed. A lone warrior on sacred land.
From the muck-filled stream spanned by splintered board

that we dare not cross, to the tracked canyon
by ancestors' hunting grounds. Running wild
with Tansy my summer's companion
half-Alsatian half-Irish Wolf Hound child

of half breeds. We stalk together against
invaders of souls and lay in the sun
sharing our lost secrets and empty angst
where are you now Tansy? Where can I run?

At a Pow Wow in Palo Alto where
I and brother Mitch WindWalker tightly embrace
Tomahawks, coup feather bound in my hair
to bless me a new name and a new place

another nation Noble Cherokee,
Phil Pleanty Nations without hanging me
by my nipples for three days, so I sway
my smudge feather to wipe that all away,
and write my rhymes with structure and grace
so I can become my age and retrace
Native American dictums impart
Cherokee warrior wisdom, let's start:
"Our first teacher is our own heart."

I spent many childhood summers on my Auntie's farm (Bopa is Welsh for Auntie). I'd run wild for hours every day with Tansy, her dog, imagining myself to be a Native American brave. I was hiding from my anguish. My dream came true at a Pow Wow in California where tribes would meet in peace to dance, sing and remember their ancestors. My blood brother, Mitch WindWalker, in a brief ceremony bestowed me with Cherokee nationhood. He gave me the most beautiful name: Phil Pleanty (sic) Nations in honour of my international family and friendships. I wear that name with pride.

The Drunken Juggler

My forbears' pain sits heavy in my heart.
In turn, ease it, soothe it with drunken sloth,
allowing the blemish I do impart.
Can I, once again, to you, plead my troth?

My body limits my domain, frees guilt,
justifies shallow, useless victimhood.
Never agrees to weeping, angered jilt,
but hush, hold me, believe; I will make good.

Understand how I am cold, full of fear.
I am alone, adrift in that dark place
with orphaned despair, loss that forms the tear
and loosens, lessens reluctant embrace.

Oh gaping gap where stood my heart and soul.
Despisèd, rejected, damaged, sealed mind,
scared, raw-skinned, dank, broken.
You can make whole,
through your bounty, and my love you will find.

So, you know, I lie, speak in blackened room,
talking, cascading sorrowful refrain.
Leap up and see beyond the harrowing gloom
and I will love you more when sometime sane.

Be still, lover, patience is all I ask.
Wretched, senseless request, you may decline.
Wait, I pause from ache to complete this task.
Imploring, humble verse; it's yours and mine.

Deserving

The looseness is so ill-fitting
I should have known
the cold chills so dampening
I should have felt
the shouting, fighting, in the orchard
in the grounds, in the sea, by the cliffs.
Climbing, and falling, over the park gates.
Gashed ankle, bleeding nose, scratched hands, naked,
noisy ambulance, laugh at the dumb strangers,
freebang buddies, quiet rage against
neglectful family.

I should have known, felt this rawness,
through this buried intelligence and loss.

So how to frame the being?
Warm to the task, warm to the truth
feeling, guiding, led by the heroes
caressing, learning, writing, in the garden,
behind the wall, on the sea, on the lake.
Smoothed, plastered, ointment-soothed, calmed,
Smile with the dumbfounded evangelists and
hug them all and all is gain.

Do Not Cry for Me

I'll cry no more
in front of the mirror
over dead-hearted stuff.
The sodden masses will
no longer suck the breath from my
gashed lungs.
Our lives can beat to a different rhythm,
care not in solitude.
Hurt blurs away.
I'll embrace the world
take you on my way.
I'll cry a poem
until the eternal eclipse
of my heart.
I'll cry forever for
You.

The Old Lovers

The dulled hearts gift
passion petals, they drift
to heavy ground,
while breathless lovers' apathetic laments
fall short of lazy ears.
Comfort slows the quickening pulse,
shrugs the fragile embrace
and tender clasp
of uncertain hands.

The thunder frights,
see flashing glory lights.
The banks of rushing streams break,
gales blow through our well-worn grasp.
Clashing cymbals announce joy unconstrained.
As our love quiets my raging, ebbing, will
rings out loud
my undying love for you.

The Sense of You

Listen
Can you hear the murmurings of love
over the crashing waves?
Can you feel
the languorous fingers deadened
by neglectful instruction
touch your soft, luminous skin and glow,
revitalised?
See me lie, so peaceful, at your side.
Your smell so sweet it clutches my heart.
You lie beside me
And whisper: "You taste delicious."
Wouldn't you go hungry, thirsty.
To savour my taste for a while longer?

SOLITUDE.

The Artist's Cor[ner]

The Power of Art

Solitude

There have been numerous articles, television programmes, discussions in creative circles about the importance and creation of art during these difficult, isolating times.

I have listened to many creative people despairing at the loss of income, activity and plans. I have also heard the opposite where artists have reverted back to their creativity to help them through crisis and been inspired by some who have picked up their brush or pen after many years absence.

Here are two poems. The first where I realise I had not appreciated so many beautiful writers, philosophers, poets, artists followed by a poem which tries to convey the healing nature of art. I hope they will bring a little light into your life as they have in mine.

Art is now.

The Artist's Lot

Hopper's solitude
Donne's clever compass
Picasso's lazy doves
Camus' bastard tree
Van Gough's bleeding ear
Tagore's forgotten garden
Hogarth's morals ha
Tao's lost way
Da Vinci's mystery
Austen's misplaced pride
Monet's war-torn lilies
Greene's drunken glory
cummings' small letters
Manet's naked lunch
Burroughs!
Goya's gruesome witches
Burgess' Droogs
Dylan's sceptical wood
Ernest's bull
Cut the heads off Wordsworth's daffodils
Magritte's pipe is a fucking pipe

The Power of Art

Anna's silhouette lingers on moist pale blue sheet, sparkles in the moonlit stark whitewashed Tuscan villa. My gaze lays on her agitated figure, flailing limbs creating shadow show on lilac walls in the shuttered cool room. I want to kiss, caress, the bump I loved from that first time. It sits above her shocking flamed pubic mound which flutters with butterfly rhythms hidden within.

I am an artist, poet, sculptor, loud, hot. I demand Anna pose on sill, still naked. I work at speed with clay that cracks sparks spins. I reproduce her distorted beauty once, twice.

Sculptures varnished, finished Anna takes one and leaves with an adieu.

I write a poem inspired by the form of the statuette.

Three months later, Anna breathlessly climbs the six flights to my sombre *chambre de bonne* I read her my poem.

She turns, leaves without a glance.

I write a poem about unrequited desires and loss, toss it, watch it go this way and that, splat inevitably in the sodden dog-shit full Parisian gutter.

"chambre de bonne" is an attic room where maids lived while serving the bourgeois apartments below. A garret.

Whole again

One month short of his 60th Birthday

The Simple Truth

Not much time

Forty Foot drop

Renaissance

To my muse

An elegy to my father

family love

father's advice

The universe pauses as infinite love expands

Julia is free

Oisín

Renaissance

Surviving the black world of depression is a re-birth. I can best sum up what this felt like for me by quoting extracts from poems I wrote many years ago to celebrate the birth of my grandchildren. And let's not forget to have some fun.

The Universe Pauses as Infinite Love Expands

π has stopped recurring.
A new angel alights atop the pin.
The rainbow acquires another hue.
I can see you through those dark walls.
I can hear you over the crashing waves of the seas.
Your scent holds me in lavender fields.

Infinite love expands for you.

An Elegy to My Father

"The Black Spider" did indeed seem to have eight limbs.

How was he so great?

Lev explained: "Have a smoke to calm your nerves before the match, then toss back a strong drink to tone your muscles."

My father, stubbing his last cigarette, tossing back a large scotch, said on the day he died:

"I met a man who complained about his painful foot. I showed him a man who had lost his leg."

Lev Ivanovich Yashin known as "The Black Spider" the greatest goalkeeper in the world, had his leg amputated when he retired from football. My father had seen him play for The Rest of the World vs England at Wembley in the 1960s.

Father's Advice

Make sure
you
have
A PLAN.

*I take
each day
as it comes.*

That is
what
I call
A PLAN.

Julia is free

Julia is free now she's got a neat Citroen still works her arse off she has a plan take each day as it comes running in the sea no tattoo features that blow you away sirens' hair loud raucous laugh spits salty gobs catches the waves throws you on the sand a smile a whisper blue eyes sweet face with no make-up floating dresses bangles so good to see Julia free

Free to give
Free to understand
Free to be a Mum
Free to be a friend
Free to wash her hair
Free to sleep twenty four hours
Free to not sleep twenty four hours
Free to have no money
Free to keep butterflies
Free to feed the kids
Free to see the dawn
Free to not smoke
Free to not drink
Free to spend
Free to pray to her God
Free to mock in Church
Free to fly
Free to sleep in her car
Free to love whomever whenever
Free to inspire poets
Free to be

she doesn't cook a meal
even though she can
and does with delicacy
never mind some tea

she is wild watch her
dancing like a crazy
woman she is free now

Julia is free

her lonely lovers have
lost her they must be in
such dark
despair…tough shit.

Family Love

I tiptoed down the wooden stair
You were hunched weeping facing away
From me over your computer screen

Keyboard pushed away
You replied to my stulted questions
'It's my cousin with the rare name who has answered me'

I listened to the truth behind those phrases
That I had heard so many times about how each
Family in the Soviet Union has lost at least one loved one

Your grandfather
Taken away as an enemy
Of the people taken away
In his big black car from
His big Party house
In Kyiv to the Gulag and shot one year later
Released
By the internet eighty years later
To force those tears to flow again

To meet your cousin in Moscow
To fall in love with me again.

To My Muse

So far we travelled
You from a different
Faraway land

Me from
Another
Unfound place

We almost met
At the end of the road

Hold on and still

Travel together

Forty Foot Drop

You don't scare me
with your
forty

       foot

              drop

I know i've only
really tried
with a

ten
  foot
       drop

But I learned

twenty

      five

          years

ago
to embrace the world

otherwise i would never have been
alone in
St. Basil's, Red Square,
Moscow.
You are still scared

I will show you:

READY?

FortyFoot

D

      R

          O

              O

                  O

                      OOOO

       PPPPPPPPPPP.

Not Much Time

I only read books that I have already read.
I only watch films that I have already seen.
I had already written this poem.

GHOTI*

Flying School
Pie battered sword
spear
fighting cat dog
blow trumpet bloat
lady lamp light
toad frog
pig parrot pearl
zebra unicorn
cow elephant pony
demoiselle jack dempsey
FIRE!!
King Jew
White gold
X-ray blue eye four eyed
TORRENT
TISH FISH TOSH!!!!

*pronounced FISH – tough, women, international: my daughters.

The Simple Truth

My heart was broken
Before I met you

There is a hole where my heart was

I tried to fill it with your love
Although your love is infinite
It is still empty

The simple truth
I have filled the hole
With the broken pieces of my heart

The healing is now
Now I can accept your love

The simple truth

I love you

One Month Short of His Sixtieth Birthday

He realised that He was one month short
of His sixtieth birthday.
He walked past the local pubs,
checking the windows,
any friends there?
finds a pub where
He knew no-one
drinks two pints of ale… quickly.
He went home, phoned His Mother.
He ate dinner with His wife.
He stripped down to His underpants
lay on the settee,
browsed one of seventeen books He was reading.
He watched TV, booked some tickets for a play,
checked the hotels for a planned holiday
later that year.
He drank some wine.
He wrote to his children, waited ten minutes; no reply.
He went to bed, fell asleep immediately.
awake in the middle of the night,
realised He had the most amazing life,
overcome with happiness.

Whole Again

All the strands have finally found
Their way homeward bound
No physical trails that you can see
But streams of consciousness; just be.

The Beginning.

Your picture — a blank page. Will you write a poem for me? You can write a poem. How did that make you feel? Why don't you write some poems? What do you feel like doing? What's the best thing about your life?

Further Reading

A Place Called Hope	Tom O'Neill Educational Printing Services 2000
Someone to Love Us	Terence O'Neill Harper Element 2010
The Choice	Edith Eger Penguin 2017